Shopify

The Ultimate Beginner's Guide

Introduction

Online shopping trend has reached new heights at present and this is expected to increase more in future. As an entrepreneur it will serve you best, if you establish your e-commerce site, irrespective of whether you own a small, medium or large business.

A well supported platform will serve as the perfect launchpad for your business, revenue and brand building. A good platform also helps streamlining existing online as well as the conventional brick and mortar shops. The success lies in choosing a platform that best suits your needs.

When it comes to using an online shopping set up platform, you have to strike a balance between flexibility and simplicity. You need to consider your specific requirements regarding the platform, and the effort and time you are ready to provide in building your online site and maintaining the site. The expected scaling up of your business is also a big influencing factor. So you have the option of having an integrated platform that is created from either the back end program you own, or use a hosted online shopping cart ecommerce solution.

If you want to succeed in your online business, other than the important considerations such as your product and marketing strategy, you need to spend some time on choosing the ideal online shopping platform. This concept has become a commonly and popularly used one in online business. When you have a well-designed online shopping platform, you can be assured of having laid the right foundation for your business to flourish.

For an online shopping platform to work for you effectively, you need to know about the features you need, the support for building your online site and the ideal option that would fit best for your business. You should consider important factors like the flexibility required for your store, the marketing and SEO support and most importantly, the budget you need to set aside for the platform set up.

The size of the store, the additional features, server support, security and the ability to manage the platform, once it is set up are other vital considerations you should not ignore at any cost. While there are several ecommerce platforms available now, only a few are worth considering. And among the valued few, Shopify is considered as the best option for new and established businesses, as it meets with almost all your ecommerce design requirements.

This eBook will take you through the various features of Shopify, the significance of using it and how best to reap profits with Shopify. You can find a comprehensive and detailed information regarding the ecommerce platform. All details in this eBook help you establish your business and direct it towards becoming a productive and revenue churning venture. Read on to master the online shopping features of Shopify and gain a competitive edge in your business.

Chapter 1: Why you need shopify

With ecommerce developing into the biggest growth influencer worldwide, it is more important than ever to choose a solution that can turn your business into a better and profitable venture. Shopify in its basic form helps to sell your products and services on the web. Here are some solid reasons as to why you need Shopify for your business.

Simplified set up

In a traditional business set up, you would need to purchase an on premise ecommerce software, which due to its standalone nature requires elaborate set up for IT and specialized development personnel, as well as management of the software. Such solutions had drawbacks like

- *Expensive*
- *Not being scalable*
- *Difficult to use*
- *Time consuming customization and integration with other processes of your business*

Further separate software componentsare needed to take care of the front end customer part of the business and the back end operations such as inventory management, order management, customer service and accounting. Bringing together the different software services to enable a comprehensive ecommerce platform hence becomes complex, with frequent need for maintenance. And this reduces overall efficiency as a result.

Luckily, Shopify provides the ideal solution by integrating all the important commerce requirements and business functions into one united platform through the SaaS model. Thus your business can create relevant, personalized and engaging online experience. This is possible with Shopify's strong infrastructure that unites all the business systems and the information which feeds the systems.

Meet with customer expectations head-on

Your business can succeed only when your target customers can buy your services and products from your store online in an easy way. Shopify is unique in the sense that it can leverage and unify both the back office and front end apps complete with their shared and unique information. This unification of all systems enables easy visibility and meet with the expectations of customers in an effective way.

Use Shopify to create your online store.

- Easy to use online store builder
- Fully customizable store design
- Trusted by 120,000+ online merchants

Start your 14-day free trial today!

Get started

Success oriented features

Some of the important requirements that shopify satisfies include

- *Unified platform: Has a unified accounting, ecommerce, inventory, POS, marketing, customer service, financials, merchandising and order management, which are managed via a platform that is cloud based.*

- *Enhanced customer centric operations: Personalized and consistent experiences for customers, targeted customer and marketing service along with a single window view of all transactions and interactions with customers at all channels and touch points.*

- *Smart order management: Increased profitability by having a single window inventory and order management throughout all supply chain and channels*

- *Personalized customer experience: Fast, unique, compelling and personalized in store, mobile and web experiences to highlight brand value and surpass customer expectations.*

- *Enable unlimited expansion: Rapid set up of sites for various business channels, models, brands, currencies, languages and countries under a single platform.*

Streamlined comprehensive approach

To manage your vital business functions, you need a platform that provides a unified solution. It should encourage collaboration, align the operational processes and offer real time visibility of data. Shopify meets with all these expectations and more. It helps control all the below functions in a cohesive manner:

- *Analyses and reporting*
- *Customer support*
- *Procurement*
- *Inventory and order management*
- *Marketing*
- *Promotions and pricing*
- *Content management*

Ecommerce platforms have moved beyond the basic unified software protocol to enable customers buy services and products easily online. Shopify has excelled in this aspect with its competitive pricing and features. The ecommerce platform helps build a business that is easy to scale, fully customizable and offers a highly automated functionality that saves time. In short, Shopify aims at providing a seamless online shopping experience across various different channels. The adaptability and flexibility provided by the software helps to maintain the pace of your business, reduce the operational expenses, boost efficiencies and completely eliminate the trouble of managing software and hardware.

Chapter 2: Simplicity at its best

Whether you have a B2B business realm or a B2C model, you need a platform that does more than the normal software functions such as transactions. A comprehensive model such as Shopify will make you competitive in the fast paced and robust markets present now. It can provide the significant advantage you need over your competitors who do not have the support of a similar technology.

Shopify supplies you with the tools you need to build your store online. Once you know the basic setup, which is easy to master, you can expect a seamless functioning of the store. And you have 24/7 phone or online support from the service. So, creating an ecommerce site for your business is just a breeze with Shopify. You will not need to know any technical codes or other background knowledge to set up your store online.

An overview of Shopify

Shopify is one of the best ecommerce shopping cart that is completely web based. With Shopify, you will be able to sell your services or goods online in an effective manner. All the aspects of an online store set up such as building a website, choosing the right design, customizing the site to fit your brand and products, managing orders and customers, tweaking the various features, receiving reports on sales, etc., are streamlined and easier to deal with, when you use Shopify.

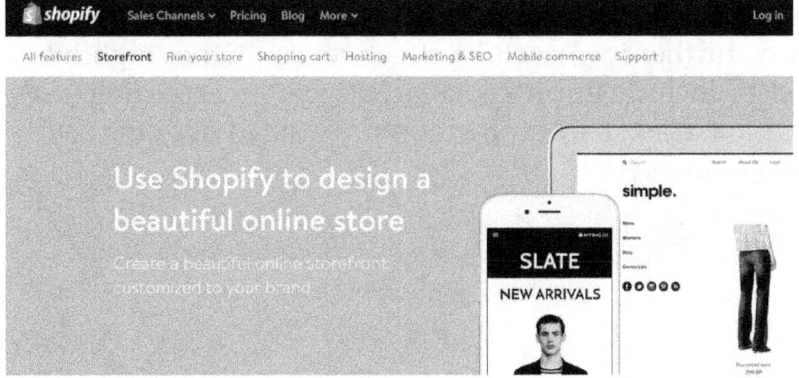

Shopify is a feature enriched sales register appropriate for small and big online retailers. The best thing about the software is you need not spend towards maintaining servers of your own, as the software is taken care of by Shopify's servers. This effectively curbs all the efforts and cost involved in server maintenance.

Founded in the year 2006, Shopify has its headquarters in Ontario, Canada. It was originally developed by Daniel Welnand, Scott Lake and Tobias Lutke for the snowboarding business they owned together. The idea for Shopify was born, when they required a shopping cart with better features than what was available at that time. They designed their own solution that met with all their requirements. The efficacy of the software made them decide on marketing it. Soon Shopify became a very popular and trusted service in the ecommerce shopping cart segment.

At present, Shopify serves over 243,000 merchants and the businesses using the service are continuously growing. Shopify has clients such as Amnesty International, Github, Foo Fighters etc. The company has done transactions that amount to more than $14 billion.

While the original version was very popular, the subsequent version Shopify 2, launched in the year 2013, surpassed the reputation of the earlier version as a highly effective ecommerce platform. The newer version had strong merchant minded and cleaner backend features. The live Theme Editor feature and the enhanced search and filter features added to the service further increased its effectiveness. Other highlights of Shopify 2 include improved analytics, better reporting tools and facility to issue part of the refunds, instead of doing the transaction via PayPal.

Convenience and simplicity

Although Shopify has numerous features in it, you need not be overwhelmed. The system is structured logically. The entire set up of your online store is easier without any complicated procedures. You will need just a few minutes to set up the basic store. Other than the designing aspect, which needs some attention because you need to balance the colors for the theme at the backend, Shopify is quite an easy to use service. Once the basic store is built, you can easily add on to it to create a fantabulous store.

Exclusive features

Some important features that make Shopify an excellent option are:

- *You can put your online store to a trial run before you launch it officially. This trial run is done in two ways. One is through a live editor feature and the other way is doing it online.*
- *To own a domain name for your store, you can do it easily via the Shopify dashboard. This is quick and easy, when compared to other services, which make it mandatory to purchase the domain via third party services.*

Customer facing or front end features

A convenient and easy to use interfaceis one of the significant features a shopping cart should have. A customer should be able to navigate through the site smoothly, select the items needed, buy them and complete the transaction successfully. If on the other hand, the process is frustrating, it will be difficult for the customer to buy a product, even if it is a good one. Thus with a difficult navigation feature, you will be left with numerous abandoned carts. And to make matters worse, customers will definitely not return to the site, nor will they recommend the store to others.

When you consider Shopify, it excels in the convenience feature. It is very easy to build a store using Shopify. Managing is also a breeze. Both in terms of administration and customer facing end, the software is easy to manage.

Customers who transact through a site backed by Shopify will feel assured about the business. They would consider the business to be a well-organized, professional and legitimate retail establishment. And one of the best and most admired part of using Shopify software is, you will not find any of its branding in your site, leaving a very consistent and great shopping experience.

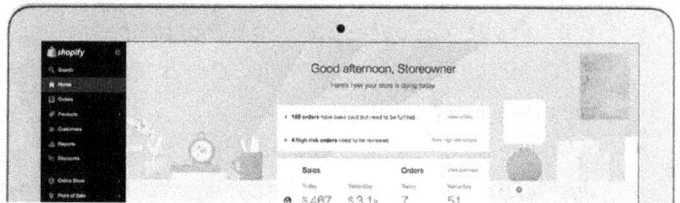

Start your free 14-day trial today!

Administration Panel or Back end management

For building your online store, you need just a few minutes. You can easily open and build the basic structure of your online store. From the beginning stage, you have the facility to preview your site, so you will know how it will look like before you launch it live. This can be done using live editor backend feature or by a password online. The password is sent to you via email, after you sign up for the free trial version.

To make the entire process easier, you are guided on the right way to use the present URL of your store. The domain set up mentioned earlier also helps a great deal. You can find this feature, when you click on the Store Settings and opt for domain.

The admin homepage provides you with four important steps. These steps help you to create the necessary groundwork, before you begin selling. These include

1. *Adding products*
2. *Customization of brand*
3. *Domain set up*
4. *Deciding on shipping and taxes information*

While these are the basic steps, there are other steps to consider too such as creating store policies, including description of your shop and the details of the product, add on features such as Google Analytics, and others.

Features such as customer information, images, items, categories and other related options are very direct and easy to understand. Partial returns and enhanced fraud detection features of the updated software version further make the software more effective.

Customer satisfaction

When it comes to shopping online, simplicity is vital. If a retail business has to invest more time on learning the basic set up and management of its store, it would start looking for an efficient and manageable shopping cart option. Shopify scores in this aspect, as it is easy to lay the groundwork with the software. The service is created in an efficient way,so you are able to tweak the features later on without having to do everything at the initial stage itself.

Outstanding user friendly features

Other than the above mentioned advantages of Shopify, here are a few more:

You can add products easily when compared to the competitors

It is easy to include links in the navigation menu for rearranging them

The article or blog section feature available with the standard Shopify format is a good one. You can add blog posts or pages easily.

Themes can be edited in a simple way.

What you need to have

As Shopify is an ecommerce software that is web based, your requirements are very simple. You need to have a proper internet connection. For the software to function smoothly, an updated and current browser such as Safar, Firefox or Chrome is necessary.

While the operating system or hardware requirements are not much elaborate, if your system has updated technology, it would facilitate easier set up of your online store. In case, you are in need of hardware addition at your physical retail store, the service has retail packages for hardware, which it supports fully.

When you go through all the convenient and easy to use features you will understand that Shopify has made its platform as easy as possible without compromising on the innovative features,which are needed for customers to have a competitive edge.

Chapter 3: Extensive template options

The company provides highly professional templates that you cannot find in other ecommerce platforms. You can find more than 100 themes, which are offered free or as paid. Paid options range from $80 and go up to $180. The design and themes featured in Shopify are stunning and elegant. The numerous free and premium templates feature themes created by big names in web design including Clearleft, Pixel Union and Happy Cog.

Setting up

Once you choose from the various themes present, the next step is to customize the feel and appearance of your site. You need to just open Shopify's template editor. The steps for editing are easy to follow, so you can make the necessary changes until you are satisfied with the look. Once you have perfected the appearance of the theme, you can upload it by visiting the Theme page. In the page you will have to click on the upload theme option. Your theme will be added. It's as simple as that!

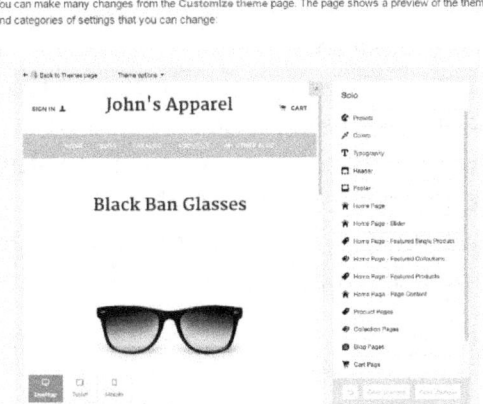

You can make many changes from the Customize theme page. The page shows a preview of the theme and categories of settings that you can change.

Website customization

At Shopify, each website template has its own individual settings. This helps you to effectively customize the design of your website. The templates have certain key concepts, which are easy to understand and help customize your site efficiently. The important concepts in the templates include

Products

These from the base unit and are the core of theme building. The feature has several subsections such as title, its description, image, price and the variants like weight, size, color etc. These and the product variants can be created and constantly updated through the online admin and the dashboard.

The variants form a powerful feature in Shopify. You can use them to display products in numerous attractive and appealing way in your templates.

Collections

After products, you need to classify them into various collections. This is necessary to categorize all the products successfully. The collections can be further organized in different ways such as alphabetically, by price, date or bestselling feature etc.

Product tags

Tags add more information to the product and help in better filtering of the collection.

Themes

Themes help to increase the appeal of the store. Shopify has over 55 themes, which are available in over 140 styles. So you can have plenty of options to choose from, when you are searching for the right theme for your online store. As mobile accounts for over 50 percent of all traffic in ecommerce, it is absolutely important for your store to be mobile responsive. Most of the themes at Shopify are of this category.

Choose a theme for your online store

Responsive themes, easily customized to fit your brand

The editor feature in theme settings allows you to preview a template as you make changes in the template. This way you can have total control over how your store will look.

Expert help

If you are in need of a completely customized template design, Shopify design experts recommend you on the ideal template set up. The service has expert developers, marketers and designers to advice on setting up a successful business online.

Without the hassles of hosting and web design limitations, Shopify provides a customer friendly admin that helps you include all you have dreamed of about your store in a template. The professional features of Shopify further help you complete the set up in a full-fledged way. And one important advantage that Shopify has with regard to its templates is, you will not find any logos or ads in the templates. You will have to look very hard to identify that the site is supported by Shopify.

Chapter 4: Best enhancing features

Shopify is an all-inclusive ecommerce platform that provides a comprehensive feature rich solution for your online store. Once you have chosen a template from the Theme store at Shopify and improve the design, you can customize and optimize your site effectively. The Liquid template language enables easy control of template optimization, even if you do not have sufficient knowledge about CSS and HTML coding. When you have optimized the template with change colors, logo and other features, you can start creating the product catalog with tools like Brand Names, Attributes, Categories and Pricing. Promotions are also easier with the promotion tool, which offers automated discounts on products at particular period of sale. After the period of promotion, the products will revert to the original price present before the sale.

Here are landmark features of Shopify

Design features

In web design, the advantages with Shopify include

- *Professional and appealing ecommerce site, which is quick to set up and starts operating in minutes*
- *Customizable and compliant with standards free templates provided with account*
- *Total control over CSS and HTML of your website.*
- *Liquid template language encourages dynamic content layout in a flexible way*
- *Facility of linking media assets to the entire shop or to individual products*
- *Forums and communities of Shopify designers to help with strategies and tips.*

Easily build and run your ecommerce website

Add products to your store, accept orders, manage website content and more

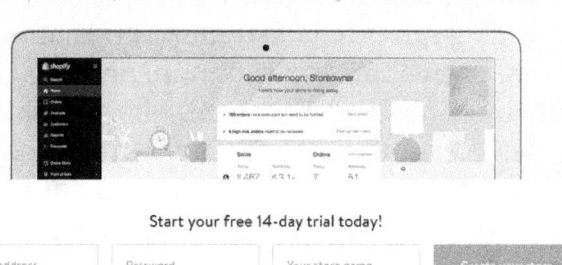

Start your free 14-day trial today!

| Email address | Password | Your store name | Create your store |

Content management features

The dynamic CMS in Shopify can help create web pages, blog posts, contact us feature and other features directly from the dashboard administration. It features SEO marketing tools and tools or coupon codes, besides having a full-fledged integral mobile commerce feature.

Order and pricing

The purchase features are highly efficient. Shopify provides secure payments via credit cards and PayPal via 50 payment channels. Customers have plenty of options for payments including eChecks, credit cards, PayPal, Google Checkout and much more.

The smart information collection features enable detection of country based on the IP address. This will result in automatic changes in the currency, tax rates, language customization in the checkout page including the checkout at the shopping cart page.

Shipping calculators are also provided with Shopify. You can set up return and refund policies with the various order processing tools enabling a streamlined checkout process.

Background features
The infrastructural features in Shopify are well designed to ensure optimal data security. The PCI compliant Level I certification makes sure that customer information is guarded safely. With its open source foundation, Shopify continues to tweak its features and improve them. The software is compatible with several direct payment systems and operates from a state of the art data center. Other salient features that reinforce the infrastructure of the ecommerce platform include

- *Ruby on Rails framework*
- *Open SBD firewall guarded Debian Linus Server hosting*
- *MySQL database support providing speed and reliability*

Point-Of-Sale
The POS feature in Shopify allows both online and physical location sales. When compared to competitors this feature has several enhanced items such as card reader, cash drawer, receipt printer and barcode scanner. All these are available for purchase as an entire package or individually, according to your requirements. With an iPad, it is possible to use Shopify effectively to

- *Sell from a stall in the market*
- *Pop up store*
- *Store in events*
- *Permanent retail outlet*

The stock and inventory are kept automatically synced with the various locations, enabling you to manage multiple stores from a single point.

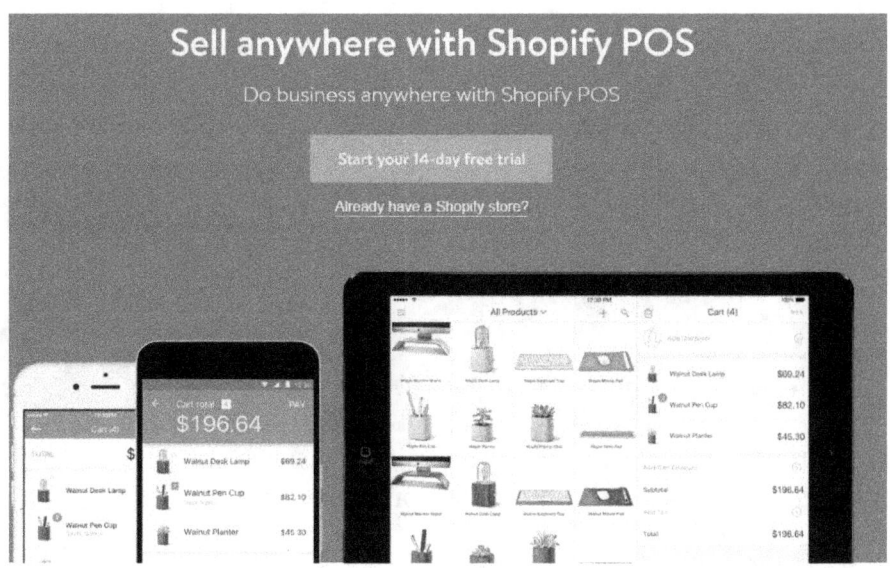

Chapter 5: Functionality augmenting apps

While the core functionality features of Shopify meet with your store requirements capably, there is another feature that can further reinforce your store's standing. The apps store at Shopify, which features both paid and free apps helps you boost your store's visibility and functions.

Shopify has more than 500 apps in its app store. Hence you are provided with plenty of options to improve the functionality of your store. Adding new products, enhancing email marketing, including customer reviews, publishing on social media, finding analytics and other such aspects are made easier with the apps present.

If you have just started using Shopify, here are some apps that will help you decide on the additions to make:

- *Data capture apps*
- *Accounting apps, which help in integrating the store with effective tools such as Quickbooks*
- *Abandoned cart saver apps, which are more innovative than the out of the box cart saver in Shopify*
- *Advanced reporting app*
- *Shopify also supports third party apps such as Freshbooks, Xero, Aweber and Zendesk*

Live chat feature can be added to improve customer support, add reviews and ratings from customers and to answer before sale questions. Visitors will be able to know the opinions of customers on the products, and adding peer reviews will further influence sales. Automation of inventory is also enhanced with such apps, eliminating the need for manual processing of orders.

You can choose the app you need for your store and ignore the apps that are not necessary. So you have full control over the entire app feature. The apps basically help to streamline business operations, save you time, effort and money, and let you focus more on the core functions effectively.

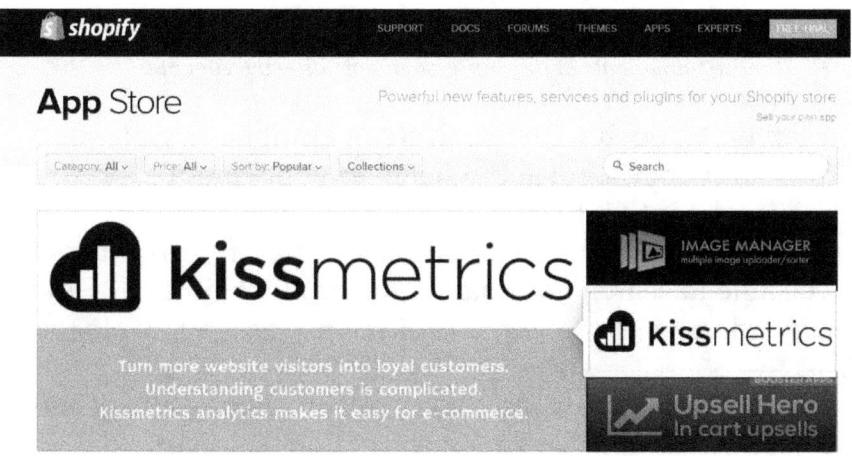

Chapter 6: Smart shopping tool

With mobile shopping taking up a huge percentage of online shopping, it is necessary for an ecommerce shopping platform to have mobile features. Shopify has robust inbuilt mobile shopping cart tools that are free, enabling users to browse and buy directly from their smart phones.

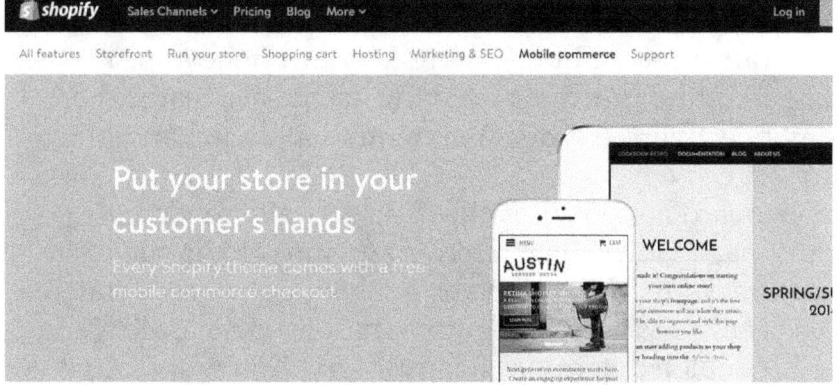

The mobile friendly features in Shopify are easy to set up and are compatible with Android phones, iPhones, and other types of smart phones. With the mobile feature, Shopify provides

- *Easy management of store via your mobile*
- *Efficient checking of customer data, sales, manage sales orders etc.*
- *Get notification on new orders as they are placed*

- *Manage inventory easily and fast*
- *Create fulfillments and capture payments directly from app*

You can be in touch with the entire operations of your store from wherever you are and whenever you want to.

Other important features

With smart shopping mobile app from Shopify, customers will be able to search for a particular product either by SKU or name, and view all the variants of the product available for sale

The mobile app feature also has an efficient customer related features such as ability to get information on a particular customer by entering the customer's name, view the address, phone number, order history and payments details. Shipping address and billing information is also easy toaccess. You need to just tap to email or call a customer enabling efficient customer support. The app also enables easy and quick switching of account directly from the menu.

Manage your store productively

With Shopify Mobile app on your smart phone, you can import your present Shopify store to your phone app. You can manage the store functions from the dashboard features on your mobile, oversee orders that require attention and other features effectively.

The dashboard also enables checking on daily revenue, referrals, page views, search terms and info on unique visitors. You can track business trends by analyzing the data available. It is also easy to take care of authorizations, open orders and replenish depleted items in the inventory. You will receive notifications on your phone instantly about orders and other information enabling better management of your store.

Chapter 7: Exemplary support

While there are several features to consider when you choose an ecommerce software such as functionality, features and pricing, support is a vital aspect that cannot be ignored. It is one of the features that can help your store sustain its growth. Shopify has some dynamic features in relation to customer service. The ecommerce software has multiple customer service support structure that helps you provide exemplary support 24/7,offering solutions for all types of ecommerce related problems that customers experience. Here are the various support types offered by Shopify:

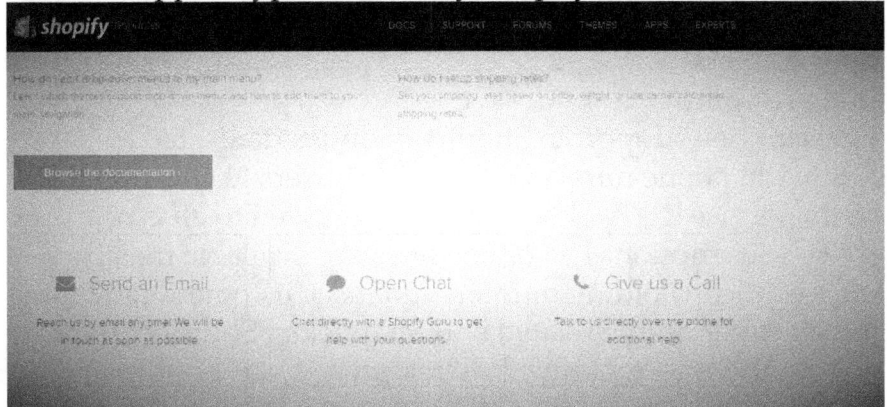

Email support

Email, even if it is considered as old fashioned way of communicating at present, is still an effective customer support channel that is used by customers. And for problems, which cannot be expressed easily in a chat or other methods, email comes in as a handy feature. Shopify support personnel are prompt in answering questions. They respond to queries within a few hours of receiving an email.

This is suggested, if you have some issue that is not urgent and in case you are in need of a detailed explanation like in relation to payment gateways or billing queries.

Live chat

This customer service feature is a very convenient one, if you need a simple and quick service. You need to just enter your query in the simple box in the site, which will link you to the support staff at Shopify. You need to enter the Shopify domain before logging to save time for the representatives, as they can identify the store the issue is present in.

Most of issues can be solved via this chat feature. If this is not possible, a representative will contact you via email to rectify the issue. This solution is ideal, if you are experiencing some technical issues that need to be rectified quickly. As technical glitches can make you lose out on the sales, these need immediate attention. A live chat can help in such instances effectively.

Phone support

The telephone support in Shopify includes dedicated worldwide phone numbers that enable users to conveniently use the service 24/7. The support is provided to all types service subscription. The phone lines are available mostly with very little holding or interruptions. Customers can talk with an expert in the related subject quickly. Shopify phone support also offers a return call features, if you need further support.

The phone support is necessary, when you have sufficient time for making the call. Most phone support enquiries are related to general queries regarding the ecommerce platform or in case you need an urgent issue that requires immediate attention.

Forums

If you need to get advice and guidance on the various features and functionality of Shopify, the Shopify Forum is the ideal place to approach. The forum helps you learn about the applications, design and other updates. If you are unable to find an answer to your query present already, you can begin a fresh thread.

This support feature is a good choice, if you need an opinion on the best application or feature for a particular aspect of your store. Forum users who have expertise in the concerned subject can provide you unbiased answers.

Manual

For detailed information on the functioning capability of Shopify, the best guide is the Shopify manual. It is meticulously created by Shopify staff and covers all information needed to use Shopify. From setting up and managing dashboard to customization and tutorials, you can find information apt for any expertise level. When you have sufficient enough time, the guide can become very useful for your store management. This is very useful to know about how the software works and when you have the Shopify POS system

E-commerce University

This is a support feature that enables you to succeed in your business. It has several useful guides, which comprehensively cover each and every aspect of your store. While being similar to the manual support this feature has additional techniques such as using social media to increase sales, finding reputed drop shipping for your business, or designing a pop up store in your locality.

This feature is very useful, if you need to have a competitive edge in your business. You can increase your skills in the fields you are not familiar or weak in including sales, product sources and marketing.

Other than the above customer support features, Shopify has also launched a support system, where customers can rate the service live. This is a highly valuable tool, which makes a customer confident of how useful his or her opinion is.

With such an enormous amount of support options, you can reach an expert at the site via phone, live chat or email. Your business will continue operating smoothly and the solid foundation provided by Shopify features further boost your business. And for those who require an ecommerce solution that contains comprehensive information, Shopify is an apt choice.

Chapter 8: Ultimate security and backup solution

Security is an important feature to consider in an ecommerce platform. Businesses need high level security to safeguard all their store information including personal data of customers. Shopify has a hosting and shopping cart with PCI compliance. The 128 bit SSL free certification is offered for all packages you get from Shopify. Complete data security is possible with the security feature without any additional cost.

Encrypt your Shopify store

Build trust with your customers and Google

Some important security features include
- *99.94 percent uptime guarantee for clients*
- *Top quality features*
- *Sufficient number of redundant power processes*
- *All around security measures*
- *Secure backups*

The monthly plan offered by Shopify includes unlimited bandwidth and hosting features. Even if your site has a huge traffic flow, you will be paying only the usually monthly package price without any additional charges.

Since hosting is taken care of by Shopify, you can concentrate on the core business functions such as managing your products, marketing etc.

Chapter 9: Reap profits with Shopify

If you are venturing into a business on the web, you can proceed in various different ways. While some opt for the self-hosting website set up, others would prefer using an ecommerce platform. Self-hosting method is difficult, if you are not well-versed with site optimization or web design. On the other hand, an ecommerce software provides you variety of choices without the need for being familiar with the technical aspects.

The right ecommerce platform should have a customizable web design, easy checkout and facility to integrate with analytics software belonging to third parties. Shopify, which is at present used by more than 25,000 stores online, is a solution that satisfies all requirements you need for an online store set up.

Excellence in Webdesign

Just as a physical store needs proper interior designing to enhance product display, you need a proper web design to ensure a successful online venture. Shopify has an amazing website wizard feature with customizable templates. You can add in all the features you need such as colors, layout, logos, fonts, slide shows and banners. So you can easily make the templates stand out and gain a competitive edge. An optimized design ensures better customer experience and more conversions, so your sales graph shows definite growth.

Streamlined management

With various management facilitating features present in a centralized dashboard, Shopify can help you manage your entire business from the dashboard. From organizing the inventory and integrating payments to managing content and marketing efforts, you can take care of all business aspects without having to spend on a separate web hosting service.

Internet marketing

The SEO features integrated in Shopify helps you to manage your content with customizable title, H1 and meta tags. You can also generate site maps automatically, so any updates on your site are reflected in the search engines immediately. You can integrate it with Google Analytics and also get a discount coupon feature that provides coupon codes for customers. Shopify has an analytics feature of its own, which help to identify the customers who have spent money in the store and utilize it for email marketing and social media campaigns. For new users $50 Facebook Advertising credits and $100 Google AdWords credits are provided, which amount to nearly five months' free service, when you buy the basic Shopify plan.

Perfect pricing

While there are several ecommerce platforms, Shopify is popular because of its competitive pricing and outstanding features. It offers highly affordable packages for small and medium businesses.

The various subscription packages at Shopify are really good. You can use the packages for any phase of your business online. For instance, if your business is just at its beginning phase and you have only a small product list, the starter plan at Shopify priced at a monthly rate of $14 allows you to list nearly 25 products, gives unlimited bandwidth and hosting of 1 GB.

Set up your shop, pick a plan later

Start your free trial

	Lite Start small without an online store	Basic Sell with your own online store	Pro Take your business to the next level	Unlimited Experience the best of Shopify
Monthly price	$9	$29	$79	$179
WAYS TO SELL				
Facebook	✓	✓	✓	✓
Shopify Buy Button	✓	✓	✓	✓
Point of Sale	✓	✓	✓	✓
Online store		✓	✓	✓

On the other hand, if you have an established product list, the regular plan at Shopify available at a monthly rate of $29, offering you unlimited products and advanced features, is a good option.

And the most favorable part is the plans do not have any hidden fees. Shopify does not require transaction fees, when you use the payment gateway at Shopify. However, this does not include the processing fees for credit card payments, which ranges from 2.25 to 2.9 percent for a transaction based on the type of plan you choose.

To run your business successfully, availing the services of Shopify will help you compete effectively in the highly challenging virtual market.

Chapter 10: How to Guide for using Shopify: Four steps to success

Shopify offers interested entrepreneurs the opportunity to test the efficacy of the ecommerce platform. It provides a 14-day free trial. Here are the steps on using Shopify to set up your online store.

1. Set up an account

To start using Shopify for your online store, you should first register with Shopify to set up an account.

Visit Shopify.com

Browse the features present

Look at the sample retail stores

For signing up, visit the home page. Scroll down and you will find the form for registration.

Enter the necessary details.

Click the green button that has, 'Create Your Store Now'option.

To name your store choose something that is unique, if not, you will be asked to select another name. Once you sign up, it will take a few minutes to set up.

Confirmation

In this step, you will be asked to enter details such as name, country, phone number and address. You should also fill in details on the products you want to sell.

If you just want to check out how Shopify works, you can enter in the Products menu option as,'I'm just having a look', and in the menu question that asks about what you want to sell, mention that you are not sure.

After entering in all the requested information click on the 'I'm done' option.

Log in

When the sign up part is completed, you will receive an email from Shopify informing about the set-up of your store. You will be provided a link to the admin page of your store along with the name of your store name at myshopify.com

Now visit the admin page using the link provided. Enter the email address you have provided in the account details and the password.

After logging in, a dashboard is provided for setting up you store.

2. Add a theme

- *Give a makeover for your virtual shop with a theme from the big collection present. This would make the store all set for stocking up the products.*
- *Browse the themes at the themes page in shopify.com. There are over 100 themes that include both free and paid themes.*
- *It is possible to filter the themes by price, industry, popularity, recent themes and features.*
- *The details about the theme and reviews on the themes will help you select the best one for your store.*
- *The reviews will help to know the experience other users had with a particular theme.*
- *Once you have selected a theme, you can add more detailed features to it such as, make it mobile responsive, or add other advanced features.*
- *Next step is previewing the theme you have selected. Click on the View Demo option present below, 'Get Theme' option.*
- *If there are different styles under a theme, you can have preview of all the various styles of the particular theme.*
- *When you have decided on the theme you want, click on 'Get Theme' green button.*
- *After confirming the theme, you should click on the 'Publish' option.*
- *Even if you are not completely certain about the theme being right for your store, you can go ahead, as it is always possible to change at a later stage.*
- *Customize the theme once it is installed by using the 'Theme Manager' option.*
- *This shows the published theme, which you had activated recently and the themes that you have previously installed.*
- *To introduce changes in fonts, colors etc. use Theme Settings option.*

3. Add Products

Once the store design is decided upon, you should start focusing on the products you want to sell. Start with adding products by using the Products option of the menu present on left side.

Now click on Add Product option.

Insert the details of the product for every product you enter. The details include

- *Name of the product*
- *Description of product*
- *Image*
- *Product type such as surf boards, games etc.*
- *Vendor such as brand name*
- *Price of product*

Other details such as taxation charges on the products, shipping address, weight of the product for shipping it etc. can also be selected and included.

SEO information of the product can also be included. There is an option for creating collections of your product, so users find it easy to search for the product they want.

The optional details that include advanced information of your product can also be opted for, if you are selling an extensive product range. The information present under this feature include,

- *SKU code, which is used to track the state of stock in the inventory*
- *Barcode refers to scannable lines, which contain information on the product*
- *Price comparison to show the low prices you charge, when compared to the competitors*

Once you have entered all the product details click on Save option. With this step, your product listing will be completed.

4.Launch your online store

Now you have completed the basic set up of your online store with Shopify. You have a great theme, product and the necessary classification.

Now the next step is to select the payment methods for your store. Fix the tax rate and shipping rate. The store settings option can be used to enter the above details. Click on 'Settings' option present in the menu.

You will have to enter the details of your credit card, when you launch the store. Billing for the service will be done once the 14-day trial period is over.

Chapter 11: How to customize Shopify to suit the needs of your store

Most of the themes in Shopify let you do simple changes, which can actually give a spectacular makeover to your store. So, you need not be worried about your store looking like a replica of the numerous other stores.

Changing the theme
Step by step instructions:

1. *Go to the admin page*
2. *In the navigation menu on left side, choose 'Themes'*
3. *Your present live theme will appear in a box with two buttons on the right side of the box.*
4. *The first button helps with the basic changes in setting. One of the changes is the facility to create a duplicate of you theme. This is a necessary step as, if you make any changes that you decide on not adding later, you can erase the duplicate and begin the tweaking again.*
5. *The second option is named Customize Theme. By clicking on this button, a page containing all basic functionality related to your store will open.*
6. *Make a detailed cover of all the settings and try out the features. This will help you know about your site's capability.*
7. *The benefits you see with the theme page include:*
   - *Upload logos and slides on to homepage carousel*
   - *Add functionality of an item to the product page*
   - *Choose the number of items you want to add to the collection page lists*

Additionally, you can reposition the page elements as you require, like make the product images appear on any part of the page. You can also decide on whether you want to add social buttons on the page or not.

How to add product

In the admin page choose Products from the menu

In the product page click on the Add a Product option.

Add the details you need to include for your product with this page. All SEO related tweaks can be done here such as description, name and the URL.

You can also add details on your product variants, so customers will know about the items you are going to sell

Upload all your product pictures in this page. Rearrange the products is easy, so you need not worry about doing them in a particular way.

Product screen

Fill out information on your product in this screen.

Since images form the main selling point of your product, display your product images in the best way possible.

Highlight the unique features with help of close up shots.

Having all images in the same dimension will help to give a neat and tidy look to your online store instead of a board on Pinterest.

Don't forget to press the Save button present in the right side of the page.

How to set up collections

A collection consists of a product group where a single or more features are common, which customers are in search of.

For instance, shopping preferences can include

- *Clothes and accessories particular to men, children and women*
- *Products that are of the same category like rugs, cushions , lamps etc. which fall under home décor*
- *Products on sale*
- *Products of a particular size, color or price*
- *Seasonal items like holiday decorations and cards*

A single product can thus appear in various different collections. The collections are usually shown in the homepage and navigation bar. Customers looking for a product can easily find it without having to browse through the entire catalog.

The screen set up for collection works similar to the product screen.

Tweaking collections

While adding a fresh collection, it is possible to remove or add a product in two ways, namely by manual method, where you include the product individually, and by automatic set up that helps you to add products that meet with particular criteria.

How to set up payment gateways

With a payment gateway, you can collect payments from the customers through your website directly. Since all payment gateway versions are not equal, you should know about the commission rate, price and the features offered in each gateway to choose appropriately.

Here are some features to look for

Transaction Fees: Look for flat fee or percentage charged by the gateways for using their service. Compare this with the sales you expect for your products and choose accordingly.

Type of card: Find out the type of cards the payment gateways accept. Most often MasterCard and Visa are accepted, and so is American Express. And PayPal is another popular payment mode that many use.

Making payment offsite

In some gateways, payment is taken using separate forms on the servers they own. The customer is led away from the checkout in your site and pays using the payment gateway sale form. Once the payment is done, the customer is redirected to the confirmation page in your store site.

This helps you to have more control on the checkout. You can check out effectively, in spite of the limitations in Shopify, which has only CSS option.

While earlier the transaction fees of the gateways were added to the fees at Shopify now just Shopify payments can be made, saving you extra expenses.

Based on the plan you choose, you can get good rates such as Unlimited plan: 1.8% + 20p

Professional plan: 2.1% + 20p

Basic plan: 2.4% + 20p

Upgrading is a good option, if you intend to make several transactions. If you reside in the UK or US, Shopify payments can be used automatically. To enable Shopify payment gateway, click on the button, 'Complete account setup' for Shopify Payments.

For using other gateway options, go to 'Enable payment gateways'option present on the same store page.

Going live with your shopify store

Before you go live and start selling online, there a few details to note about the deliveries, payment of taxes and other details of you company.

Ensure you have all information related to your business is filled on the General business page. Include Google Analytics to track the visitors to your store and increase the sales.

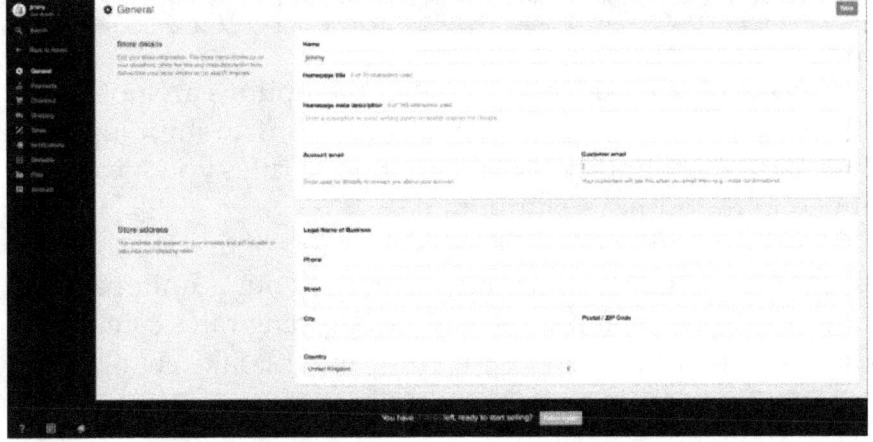

Taxes

Visit the product page in your admin

Choose a given product

Navigate to Inventory and variants section

Now click on edit link present next to Product Variant

This will open a dialogue window.

Check the Shipping and taxes boxes, if these are needed for your product. Digital goods for instance, do not need shipping or taxes, but a clothing store would need both.

If you are shipping, make sure you have the weight of the product entered in a suitable field.

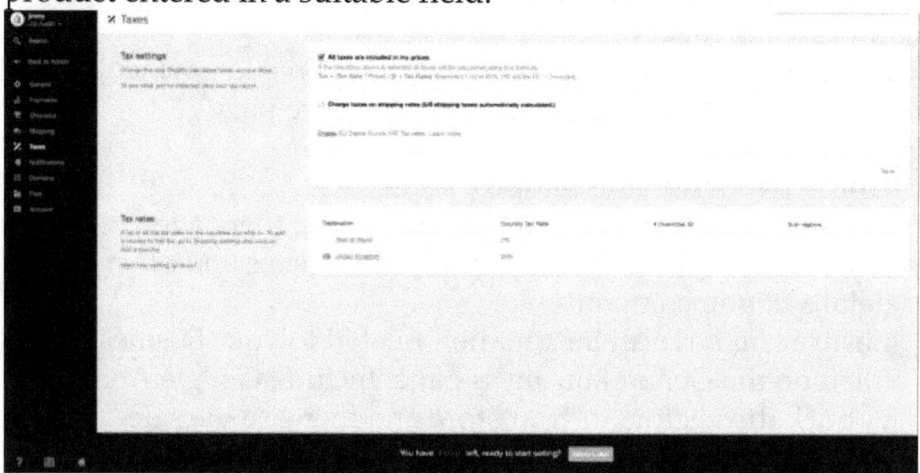

Tips on shipping

If you have narrow shipping rates or the options are not sufficient, it may lead to a drop in the sales. The shipping rate is calculated by Shopify based only on the rules you have defined in the admin's shipping page.

To ensure you do not miss sales on account of this factor, go to the shipping page in the settings menu of your admin page. Adjust the prices you have set in the shipping rates category. Ensure whether the rate is based on weight. Make changes based on the specifications of your product.

Test trial the order system

The Bogus Gateway of Shopify is a very useful tool, to check whether your order system is working well. This gateway simulates a transaction.

Here are the steps to follow:

Go to the admin page of your store

Click on Payment option in the Settings menu

Deactivate any credit card payment gateway before you continue. This can be done by using the edit button, choosing deactivate, and confirming it.

Open the drop down menu option by choosing one of the credit card gateways in the credit card section

Find the Bogus Gateway option in the menu and choose it.

Click on Activate option. If you had already used the Bogus method, choose reactivate.

Visit your store and do the steps just as a customer does when placing an order.

Test trial with genuine transaction

Ensure you have the required payment gateway set up properly.

Use genuine credit card details and purchase like a real customer

Cancel your order immediately to avoid paying transaction fees and to refund the money

Make sure the payment funds passed through by logging in to the payment gateway.

If you do not cancel and request a refund, the transaction fees will be seen in your bill.

This can be still cancelled, but the funds will be received as transaction credit in your Shopify bill.

You can pay any future transaction fees with this credit.

Use the transaction credits to pay any future transaction fees.

Setting up a Domain

A domain name is necessary, if you want to make your site live. This can be done in two ways.

If you want to save time and have no prior knowledge about website hosting, the best option is to buy a domain directly from Shopify. The domain will automatically be added on your store. The domains cost from $9 to $14 annually. Another option is to use a third party site like GoDaddy to buy the domain. The price range starts from $1.99 per year. But in this option, you need to do redirection of DNS records on your own, which is a bit daunting at the beginning.

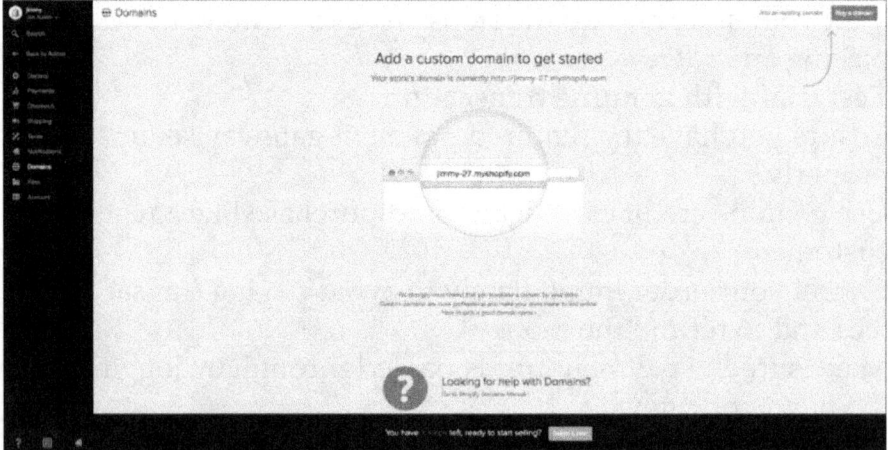

Here is a step by step guide to use domain from a third party on Shopify

1. *Go to the Settings option in the admin menu and choose Domains.*

2. *Add the domain name with 'Add an existing domain' option.*

3. *Login to the domain registrar and add the following changes to DNS records*

4. *Replace main A or @ record using the IP address: - 23.227.38.32*

5. *Replace or add storename.myshopify.com (your Shopify store link without http part) to the www CNAME*

6. *Delete storefront passwords to enable customers to access your site easily.*

7. *If relevant, set a primary domain. This can be enabled by using drop down menu at the Domains section of Settings in your admin page.*

8. *Also check the box that redirects all traffic to the primary domain. This will give good SEO for your store.*

Other domain additions

By repeating steps 1-5, you can include other domain names and have them directed to the main primary domain. The primary can be changed whenever you need by using the steps 7 and 8.

Your store's SEO will not be influenced by the multiple domain names you own, so adding more domain names is not necessary.

As you can see, setting up a Shopify store and customizing it is very easy. You can make your entire store functional in just less than 30 minutes, without having any expert knowledge on website set up. Now the next step is promoting your product.

Chapter 12: How to effectively promote your Shopify Store

It is easy to increase the conversions and sales in your Shopify store, if you know how to promote the store. Several online marketing methods can be used for achieving this goal. Here are some easy strategies that help to get your store top rankings in the search engine and increase traffic to your online store.

Social media icons

Add and promote all social networks you have set up a profile in via your website, marketing materials and blog. You can attract more number of users who will follow you on the social networks they frequent.

Moreover this method helps users to advertise your website on their social networks.

Feature in listings of local businesses

Have your site appear in the directories of local businesses such as Google Places or Yahoo Local. You will receive links and also connect successfully with your local customers.

Consider Blogging

Having a blog is highly advantageous, as it helps in link building particularly when you post relevant and interesting content. This will attract natural links and subscribers. Make sure to post frequently.

Make use of Affiliate links

You can use other marketers to increase sales in your business via affiliate programs. Affiliate links are provided to marketers, so you can track and give them a commission. But all the affiliate links do not increase SEO. When you use proper software for affiliate programs, you can get great SEO benefits.

Lure with discounts

Discounts help in increasing sales and link building chances. Try offering discounts to non-profits, charities and schools. Such links help to boost your site's rankings.

Create an email list

The main focus of your store should be on building a strong connection with customers and make them buy repeatedly. By sending messages to them frequently you can accomplish this. Having an email list will help you send messages to target customers.

Try offering free guide connected to your special niche or use valuable information to promote a newsletter or send emails that stress on discounts, giveaways and deals to entice potential users to give their contact information enabling you to send future emails to them easily.

Use the Facebook friends list to build the customer list and upload the list on Mail Chimp or Aweber. A pop up email with the Shopify plugin can be used, or a newsletter signup can be offered with the guide.

Communities and events

Use networking events to form new connections and turn them into customers. Sites such as Meetup.com, Eventbrite.com and the various social media networks can be used this way.

With the above measures you can build a stronger connection with your customers and increase your sales and reach successfully.

Conclusion

Starting an online business needs an efficient ecommerce software. When you choose an ideal software, it can make it easier to build your website and manage it. You can efficiently automate all the operations and focus on increasing your customers and sales. Shopify is a perfect ecommerce software, which offers all requirements of managing a store online including web design, hosting, payment processing, merchant tools and various other capabilities.

At a time when ecommerce platforms are vying to offer the most advanced but complicated solutions, Shopify attracts users with is simplified shopping cart design. While being simplified, it does not compromise on the essential features. And Shopify eliminates the hassles of having to deal with self-hosting, maintaining servers and other time consuming functions. The auxiliary apps help in enhancing the entire store set up from the management of inventory to contacting customers during and after the sale.

Thus, entrepreneurs availing the services of Shopify can rest assured that they can have their entire attention on their core business function, instead of having to deal with the hassles of website building and management of shopping cart.

And with Shopify you can forget about lag or downtime. All upgrades and maintenance are taken care of expertly by Shopify. The ecommerce platform has an impressive list of clients to attest its reliability such as General Electric, Cross Fit, Amnesty International, Tesla Motors and more. It has the required infrastructure to deal with your business cost-effectively and reliably. It believes in simplified management of your business. With so many advantageous factors, making use of Shopify for your online business will be the most prudent and profit churning decision you will make.

www.ingramcontent.com/pod-product-compliance
Lightning Source LLC
Chambersburg PA
CBHW070416190526
45169CB00003B/1287